Bariatric Diet Cookbook

For Beginners

Emily Sparker

Table of Contents

Oatmeal Casserole

Preparation time:

10 minutes Cooking time: 20 minutes

Ingredients:

- 2 cups rolled oats
- 1 teaspoon baking powder 1/3 cup brown sugar
- 1 teaspoon cinnamon powder
- ½ cup chocolate chips 2/3 cup blueberries
- 1 banana, peeled and mashed 2 cups milk
- eggs
- tablespoons butter
- 1 teaspoon vanilla extract

Instructions:

- In a bowl, mix sugar with baking powder, cinnamon, chocolate chips, blueberries and banana and stir.

- In a separate bowl, mix eggs with vanilla extract and butter and stir. Heat up your air fryer at 320 degrees F, grease with cooking spray and add oats on the bottom.

- Add cinnamon mix and eggs mix, toss and cook for 20 minutes. Stir one more time, divide into bowls and serve for breakfast.

Nutrition Facts:

calories 300, fat 4, fiber 7, carbs 12, protein 10

Ham Breakfast

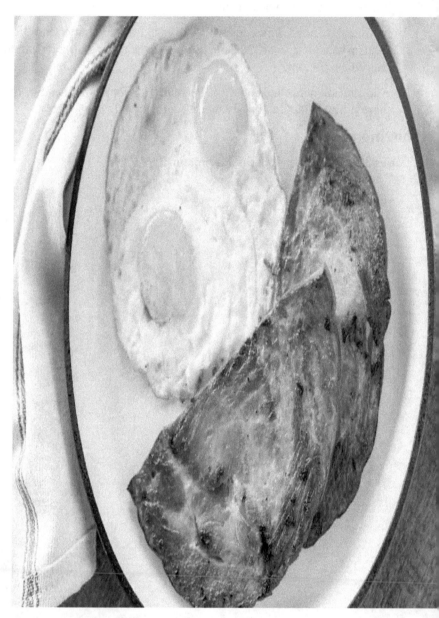

Preparation time:

10 minutes Cooking time: 15 minutes

Ingredients:

- 6 cups French bread, cubed
- 4 ounces green chilies, chopped 10 ounces ham, cubed
- ounces cheddar cheese, shredded 2 cups milk
- eggs
- 1 tablespoon mustard
- Salt and black pepper to the taste

Instructions:

- Heat up your air fryer at 350 degrees F and grease it with cooking spray. In a bowl, mix eggs with milk, cheese, mustard, salt and pepper and stir.

- Add bread cubes in your air fryer and mix with chilies and ham. Add eggs mix, spread and cook for 15 minutes.

Nutrition Facts:

calories 200, fat 5, fiber 6, carbs 12, protein 14

Tomato and Bacon Breakfast

Preparation time:

10 minutes Cooking time: 30 minutes

Ingredients:

- 1 pound white bread, cubed
- 1 pound smoked bacon, cooked and chopped ¼ cup olive oil 1 yellow onion, chopped
- 28 ounces canned tomatoes, chopped
- ½ teaspoon red pepper, crushed
- ½ pound cheddar, shredded
- 2 tablespoons chives, chopped
- ½ pound Monterey jack, shredded 2 tablespoons stock
- Salt and black pepper to the taste 8 eggs, whisked

Instructions:

- Add the oil to your air fryer and heat it up at 350 degrees F. Add bread, bacon, onion, tomatoes, red pepper and stock and stir.

- Add eggs, cheddar and Monterey jack and cook everything for 2 minutes.

- Divide among plates, sprinkle chives and serve.

Nutrition Facts:

calories 231, fat 5, fiber 7, carbs 12, protein 4

Tasty Hash

Preparation time:

10 minutes Cooking time: 15 minutes

Ingredients:

- 16 ounces hash browns
- ¼ cup olive oil
- ½ teaspoon paprika
- ½ teaspoon garlic powder
- Salt and black pepper to the taste 1 egg, whisked
- 2 tablespoon chives, chopped 1 cup cheddar, shredded

Instructions:

- Add oil to your air fryer, heat it up at 350 degrees F and add hash brown
- Also add paprika, garlic powder, salt, pepper and egg, toss and cook frl5 minutes.
- Add cheddar and chives, toss, divide among plates and serve.

Nutrition Facts:

calories 213, fat 7, fiber 8, carbs 12, protein 4

Creamy Hash Browns

Preparation time:

10 minutes Cooking time: 20 minutes

Ingredients:

- 2 pounds hash browns 1 cup whole milk
- 8 bacon slices, chopped 9 ounces cream cheese 1 yellow onion, chopped
- 1 cup cheddar cheese, shredded 6 green onions, chopped
- Salt and black pepper to the taste 6 eggs
- Cooking spray

Instructions:

- Heat up your air fryer at 350 degrees F and grease it with cooking spray.

- In a bowl, mix eggs with milk, cream cheese, cheddar cheese, bacon, onion, salt and pepper and whisk well.

- Add hash browns to your air fryer, add eggs mix over them and cook for 20 minutes.

Nutrition Facts:

calories 261, fat 6, fiber 9, carbs 8, protein 12

Blackberry French Toast

Preparation time:

10 minutes Cooking time: 20 minutes

Ingredients:

- 1 cup blackberry jam, warm 12 ounces bread loaf, cubed
- 8 ounces cream cheese, cubed 4 eggs
- 1 teaspoon cinnamon powder 2 cups half and half
- ½ cup brown sugar
- 1 teaspoon vanilla extract

Instructions:

- grease your air fryer with cooking spray and heat it up at 300 degrees F. Add blueberry jam on the bottom, layer half of the bread cubes, then add cream cheese and top with the rest of the bread.

- In a bowl, mix eggs with half and half, cinnamon, sugar and vanilla, whisk well and add over bread mix.

- Cook for 20 minutes, divide among plates and serve for breakfast.

Nutrition Facts:

calories 215, fat 6, fiber 9, carbs 16, protein 6

Smoked Sausage Breakfast Mix

Preparation time:

10 minutes Cooking time: 30 minutes

Ingredients:

- 1 and ½ pounds smoked sausage, chopped and browned A pinch of salt and black pepper

- 1 and ½ cups grits 4 and ½ cups water

- 16 ounces cheddar cheese, shredded 1 cup milk

- ¼ teaspoon garlic powder

- 1 and ½ teaspoons thyme, chopped Cooking spray

- 4 eggs, whisked

Instructions:

- Put the water in a pot, bring to a boil over medium heat, add grits, stir, cover, cook for 5 minutes and take off heat. Add cheese, stir until it melts and mix with milk, thyme, salt, pepper, garlic powder and eggs and whisk really well.
- Heat up your air fryer at 300 degrees F, grease with cooking spray and add browned sausage.
- Add grits mix, spread and cook for 25 minutes. Divide among plates and serve for breakfast.

Nutrition Facts:

calories 321, fat 6, fiber 7, carbs 17, protein 4

Air Fryer Breakfast Sausage

Prep Time:

10 Minutes Cook Time: 10 Minutes Total Time: 20 Minutes

Ingredients:

- lb ground pork 1 lb ground turkey 2 tsp fennel seeds
- tsp dry rubbed sage 2 tsp garlic powder
- 1 tsp paprika 1 tsp sea salt
- 1 tsp dried thyme
- 1 tbsp real maple syrup

Instructions:

- Begin by mixing the pork and turkey in a large bowl. In a small bowl, mix the remaining Ingredients fennel, sage, garlic powder, paprika, salt, and thyme. Pour spices into the meat and continue to mix until the spices are completely incorporated.

- Spoon into balls (about 2-3 tbsp of meat), and flatten into patties. Place inside the air fryer, you will probably have to do this in 2 batches.

- Set the temperature to 370 degrees, and cook for 10 minutes. Remove from the air fryer and repeat with the remaining sausage.

Nutritional Value

Calories: 68kcal Carbohydrates: 13g Protein: 2g

Fat: 1g

Sodium: 400g

Crispy Bacon In The Air Fryer

Prep Time:

0 Minutes Cook Time: 10 Minutes Total Time: 10 Minutes

Ingredients:

- 1 Pound of Bacon

Instructions:

- Add bacon into the air fryer basket, evenly. This may take 2 batches to cook all of the bacon, depending on size.

- Cook at 350 degrees for 5 minutes.

- Turn bacon and cook an additional 5 minutes or until your desired crispiness.

- Remove bacon with tongs and place on a paper towel-lined plate. Let cool and serve.

Nutrition Information:

Calories:177|Totalfat:33g|Saturatedfat:5g|Transfat:0g|Cholesterol:37mg| 637mg|Carbohydrates: 1g|Sugar: 0g|Protein: 13g

Air Fryer Breakfast Stuffed Peppers

Prep Time:

5 minutes Cook Time: 13 minutes Total Time: 18 minutes Servings: 2

Ingredients:

- 1 bell pepper halved, middle seeds removed 4 eggs
- 1 tsp olive oil
- 1 pinch salt and pepper
- 1 pinch sriracha flakes for a bit of spice, optional

Instructions:

- Cut bell peppers in half lengthwise and remove seeds and middle leaving the edges intact like bowls.

- Use your finger to rub a bit of olive oil just on the exposed edges (where it was cut).

- Crack two eggs into each bell pepper half. Sprinkle with desired spices. Set them on a trivet inside your Ninja Foodi or directly inside your other brand of the air fryer.

- Close the lid on your air fryer (the one attached to the Ninja Foodi machine).

- Turn the machine on, press the air crisper button at 390 degrees for 13 minutes (times will vary slightly according to how well done you like your egg but this was perfect for us).

- Alternatively, if you'd rather have your bell pepper and eggless brown on the outside add just one egg to your pepper and set the air fryer to 330 degrees for 15 minutes. (for an over hard egg consistency)

Nutrition Facts:

Fat: 10g Saturated Fat: 3g

Cholesterol: 327mg Sodium: 146mg Potassium: 246mg Carbohydrates: 4g Fiber: 1g

Sugar: 2g Protein: 11g Vitamin C: 76mg Calcium: 49mg Iron: 1.8mg

Fryer Bacon And Egg Breakfast Biscuit Bombs

Prep Time:

35 Mins Cook Time: 15 Mins Total: 50 MIN

Ingredients:

- Biscuit Bombs
- slices bacon, cut into 1/2-inch pieces 1 tablespoon butter
- 2 eggs, beaten
- 1/4 teaspoon pepper
- can (10.2 oz) Pillsbury Grands! Southern Homestyle refrigerated Buttermilk biscuits (5 biscuits)
- z sharp cheddar cheese, cut into ten 3/4-inch cubes Egg Wash
- 1 egg
- 1 tablespoon water

Instruction:

- Prevent your screen from going dark while you cook.

- Cut two 8-inch rounds of cooking parchment paper. Place one round ϵ bottom of the air fryer basket. Spray with cooking spray.

- In 10-inch nonstick skillet, cook bacon over medium-high heat until crisp. Remove from pan; place on paper towel. Carefully wipe skillet with a paper towel. Add butter to skillet; melt over medium heat. Add beaten eggs and pepper to skillet; cook until eggs are thickened but sti moist, stirring frequently. Remove from heat; stir in bacon. Cool 5 minutes.

- Meanwhile, separate dough into 5 biscuits; separate each biscuit into 2 layers. Press each into a 4-inch round. Spoon 1 heaping tablespoonful of egg mixture onto the center of each round. Top with one piece of cheese. Gently fold edges up and over filling; pinch to seal. In a small bowl, beat the remaining egg and water. Brush biscuits on all sides wi egg wash.

- Place 5 of the biscuit bombs, seam sides down, on parchment in the ai fryer basket. Spray both sides of the second parchment round with cooking spray. Top biscuit bombs in a basket with a second parchmen

- round, then top with remaining 5 biscuit bombs.

- Set to 325°F; cook 8 minutes. Remove top parchment round; using tongs, carefully turn biscuits, and place in basket in a single layer. Cook 4 to 6 minutes longer or until cooked through (at least 165°F).

Nutrition Information::

Calories: 200 Total Fat: 12g

Saturated Fat: 6g

Cholesterol: 85mg Sodium: 440mg Potassium: 50mg

Total Carbohydrate: 17g Sugars: 3g

Protein: 7g

Air Fryer Sausage Breakfast Casserole

Prep Time:

10 Minutes Cook Time: 20 Minutes Total Time: 30 Minutes

Ingredients:

- 1 Lb Hash Browns
- 1 Lb Ground Breakfast Sausage 1 Green Bell Pepper Diced
- 1 Red Bell Pepper Diced
- 1 Yellow Bell Pepper Diced 1/4 Cup Sweet Onion Diced 4 Eggs

Instructions:

- Foil line the basket of your air fryer. Place the hash browns on the bottom. Top it with the uncooked sausage.

- Evenly place the peppers and onions on top. Cook on 355* for 10 minutes.

- Open the air fryer and mix up the casserole a bit if needed. Crack each egg in a bowl, then pour right on top of the casserole. Cook on 355* for another 10 minutes.

- Serve with salt and pepper to taste.

Nutrition Information::

Calories:517|Totalfat:37g|Saturatedfat:10g|Transfat:0g|Cholesterol:227m 1092mg|Carbohydrates:27g|Sugar: 4g|Protein: 21g

Air Fryer Baked Egg Cups w/ Spinach & Cheese

Prep Time:

5 mins Cook Time: 10 mins Total Time: 15 mins

Ingredients:

- 1 large egg
- 1 tablespoon (15 ml) milk or half & half
- 1 tablespoon (15 ml) frozen spinach, thawed (or sautéed fresh spinach)
  1-2 teaspoons (5 ml) grated cheese
- Salt, to taste
- Black pepper, to taste
- Cooking spray, for muffin cups or ramekins

Instructions:

- Spray inside of silicone muffin cups or ramekin with oil spray. Add egg, milk, spinach, and cheese into the muffin cup or ramekin.

- Season with salt and pepper. Gently stir ingredients into egg whites without breaking the yolk.

- Air Fry at 330°F for about 6-12 minutes (single egg cups usually take about 6 minutes - multiple or doubled up cups take as much as 12. As you add more egg cups, you will need to add more time.)

- Cooking in a ceramic ramekin may take a little longer. If you want runny yolks, cook for less time. Keep checking the eggs after 5 minute to ensure the egg is to your preferred texture.

Nutrition Facts:

Calories: 115kcal | Carbohydrates: 1g | Protein: 10g | Fat: 7g | Saturated Fat 2g | Cholesterol: 216mg | Sodium: 173mg | Potassium: 129mg | Sugar 1g | Vitamin A: 2040IU | Calcium: 123mg | Iron: 1.3mg

Airfryer French Toast Sticks Recipe

Prep Time:

5 minutes Cook Time: 12 minutes Total Time: 17 minutes

Ingredients:

- 4 pieces bread (whatever kind and thickness desired) 2 Tbsp butter (or margarine, softened)
- 2 eggs (gently beaten) 1 pinch salt
- 1 pinch cinnamon
- 1 pinch nutmeg
- 1 pinch ground cloves
- 1 tsp icing sugar (and/or maple syrup for garnish and serving)

Instructions:

- Preheat Airfryer to 180* Celsius.

- In a bowl, gently beat together two eggs, a sprinkle of salt, a few heavy shakes of cinnamon, and small pinches of both nutmeg and ground cloves.

- Butter both sides of bread slices and cut into strips.

- Dredge each strip in the egg mixture and arrange it in Airfryer (you will have to cook in two batches).

- After 2 minutes of cooking, pause the Airfryer, take out the pan, making sure you place the pan on a heat-safe surface and spray the bread with cooking spray.

- Once you have generously coated the strips, flip and spray the second side as well.

- Return pan to the fryer and cook for 4 more minutes, checking after a couple of minutes to ensure they are cooking evenly and not burning.

- When the egg is cooked and the bread is golden brown, remove it from Airfryer and serve immediately.

- To garnish and serve, sprinkle with icing sugar, top with whip cream, drizzle with maple syrup, or serve with a small bowl of syrup for dipping.

Nutrition Facts:

Calories:178Kcal|Totalfat:15g|Saturatedfat:8g|Transfat:12g|Cholesterol:

193mg|Carbohydrates: 2g|Sugar: 1g|Protein: 5g| Iron: 0.8mg| Calcium: 25mg

Air Fryer Breakfast Frittata

Prep Time:

15 mins Cook Time: 20 mins Total Time: 35 mins

Ingredients:

- ¼ pound breakfast sausage fully cooked and crumbled 4 eggs, lightly beaten
- ½ cup shredded Cheddar-Monterey Jack cheese blend 2 tablespoons red bell pepper, diced
- 1 green onion, chopped
- 1 pinch cayenne pepper (Optional) cooking spray

Direction:

- Combine sausage, eggs, Cheddar-Monterey Jack cheese, bell pepper. onion, and cayenne in a bowl and mix to combine.

- Preheat the air fryer to 360 degrees F (180 degrees C). Spray a nonstick 6x2-inch cake pan with cooking spray.

- Place egg mixture in the prepared cake pan.

- Cook in the air fryer until frittata is set, 18 to 20 minutes.

Nutrition Facts:

Calories: 380| Protein 31.2g| Carbohydrates 2.9g| Fat 27.4g| Cholesterol 443mg| Sodium 693.5mg| Vitamin A Iu: 894.6IU|Vitamin B6: 0.3mg|Vitamin C:

13.4mg|Calcium:69.2mg|Iron:3mg|Magnesium:26.7mg|Potassium:328.4mg| Sodium: 693.5mg|Thiamin: 0.1mg

Breakfast Potatoes In The Air Fryer

Prep Time:

2 minutes Cook Time: 15 minutes Total Time: 17 minutes Servings: 2

Ingredients:

- 5 medium potatoes, peeled and cut to 1-inch cubes (Yukon Gold work best)
- 1 tbsp oil
- Breakfast Potato Seasoning 1/2 tsp kosher salt
- 1/2 tsp smoked paprika 1/2 tsp garlic powder
- 1/4 tsp black ground pepper

Instructions:

- Preheat the air fryer for about 2-3 minutes at 400F degrees. This will give you the crispiest potatoes.

- Meanwhile, toss the potatoes with breakfast potato seasoning and oil until thoroughly coated.

- Spray the air fryer basket with a nonstick spray. Add the potatoes and cook for about 15 minutes, stopping and shaking the basket 2-3 times throughout to promote even cooking.

- Transfer to a plate and serve right away.

Nutrition Facts:

Calories: 375 Fat: 7g Sodium: 635mg

Potassium: 2199mg63 Carbohydrates: 67g Fiber: 13

Protein: 13g Vitamin A: 245IU Vitamin: C 60.7mg Calcium: 160mg Iron: 17.4mg

Air-Fried Breakfast Bombs Are A Portabl
Healthy Meal

Prep Time:

20 Mins Total Time: 25 Mins Yield: Serves 2

Ingredients:

- 3 center-cut bacon slices

- 3 large eggs, lightly beaten

- 1 ounce 1/3-less-fat cream cheese, softened 1 tablespoon chopped fre
  chives

- 4 ounces fresh prepared whole-wheat pizza dough Cooking spray

Instructions:

How To Make It Step 1

- Cook bacon in a medium skillet over medium until very crisp, about 10 minutes. Remove bacon from pan; crumble. Add eggs to bacon drippings in pan; cook, stirring often, until almost set but still loose, about 1 minute. Transfer eggs to a bowl; stir in cream cheese, chives, and crumbled bacon.

Step 2

- Divide dough into 4 equal pieces. Roll each piece on a lightly floured surface into a 5-inch circle. Place one-fourth of the egg mixture in the center of each dough circle. Brush outside edge of dough with water; wrap dough around egg mixture to form a purse, pinching together dough at the seams.

Step 3

- Place dough purses in a single layer in an air fryer basket; coat well with cooking spray. Cook at 350°F until golden brown, 5 to 6 minutes, checking after 4 minutes.

Nutritional Information

Calories: 305 Fat: 15g

Sat fat: 5g Unsatfat: 8g Protein: 19g Carbohydrate: 26g Fiber: 2g

Sugars: 1g Added sugars: 0g Sodium: 548mg

Air Fryer Scrambled Eggs

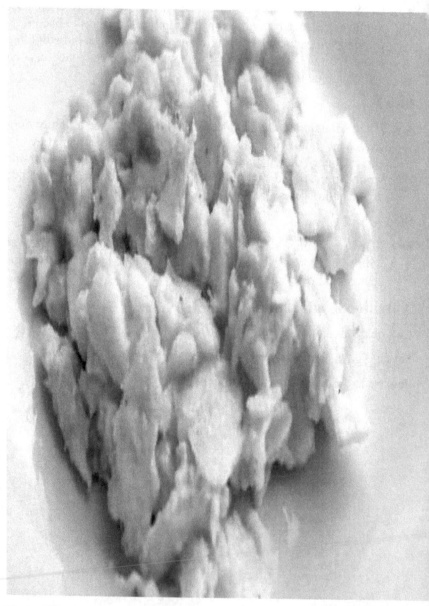

Prep Time:

3 Minutes Cook Time: 9 Minutes Total Time: 12 Minutes

Ingredients:

- 1/3 tablespoon unsalted butter 2 eggs
- 2 tablespoons milk Salt and pepper to taste 1/8 cup cheddar cheese

Instructions:

- Place butter in an oven/air fryer-safe pan and place inside the airfryer. Cook at 300 degrees until butter is melted, about 2 minutes.

- Hisk together the eggs and milk, then add salt and pepper to taste. Place eggs in a pan and cook it at 300 degrees for 3 minutes, then pus eggs to the inside of the pan to stir them around.

- Cook for 2 more minutes then add cheddar cheese, stirring the eggs again.

- Cook 2 more minutes.

- Remove pan from the air fryer and enjoy them immediately.

Nutrition Information:

Calories:126Kcal|Totalfat:9g|Saturatedfat:4g|Transfat:0g|Choleste

ol200 275mg|Carbohydrates: 1g|Sugar: 1g|Protein: 9g| Iron: 0.8mg| Calcium: 4mg

Air Fryer Banana Bread

Prep Time:

10 minutes Cook Time: 28 minutes Total Time: 38 minutes Servings: 8

Ingredients:

- 3/4 c all-purpose flour 1/4 tsp baking soda 1/4 tsp salt

- egg

- bananas overripe, mashed 1/2 tsp vanilla

- 1/4 c sour cream 1/4 c vegetable oil 1/2 c sugar

- 7" bundt pan

Instructions:

- Mix dry ingredients in one bowl and wet in another. Slowly combine the two until flour is incorporated, do not overmix.

- Spray inside of 7" bundt pan with nonstick spray and pour in batter. Place inside air fryer basket and close. Set to 310 degrees for 28 minutes.

- Remove when done and allow to sit in the pan for 5 minutes. Then gently flip over on a plate. Drizzle melted frosting on the top, slice, a serve.

Nutrition Facts:

Calories: 198 Fat: 9g Saturated Fat: 7g

Cholesterol: 24mg Sodium: 121mg Potassium: 136mg Carbohydrates: 28 Fiber: 1g

Sugar: 16g

Protein 2g Vitamin A: 93IU Vitamin C: 3mg Calcium: 14mg Iron: 1mg

Easy Air Fryer Breakfast Frittata

Prep Time:

5 min Cook Time: 10 min Total Time: 15 minutes Yield: 4 servings

Ingredients:

- 4 eggs
- ½ cup shredded sharp cheddar cheese
- ¼ cup fresh spinach, chopped 2 scallions, chopped
- 2 tablespoons half and half salt and pepper to taste

Instructions:

- In a medium bowl, beat eggs with half and half. Stir in cheese, spinach, scallions, salt, and pepper.

- Spray a 6″ cake pan with cooking spray (very important). Pour mixture into the pan.

- Air fry at 350 degrees (F) for 10-14 minutes. A toothpick inserted will come out clean when done.

- Let cool for 5 minutes before removing from pan and serving.

Nutritional Value

Calories:178Kcal|Totalfat:15g|Saturatedfat:8g|Transfat:12g|Cholesterol: 193mg|Carbohydrates: 2g|Sugar: 1g|Protein: 5g| Iron: 0.8mg| Calcium: 25mg

Air Fryer Breakfast Pizza

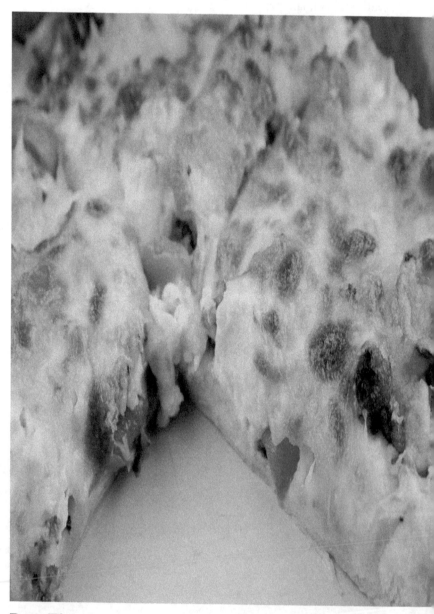

Prep Time:

5 Minutes Cook Time: 15 Minutes Total Time: 20 Minutes

Ingredients:

- Crescent Dough 3 scrambled eggs crumbled sausage
- 1/2 chopped pepper 1/2 cup cheddar cheese
- 1/2 cup mozzarella cheese

Instructions:

- Spray Pan with oil, Spread dough in the bottom of a Fat daddio or springform pan. Place in the air fryer on 350 for 5 minutes or until the top is slightly brown

- Remove from the air fryer . Top with Eggs, sausage, peppers, and cheese, Or use your favorite toppings.

- Place in the air fryer for an additional 5-10 minutes or until the top is golden brown.

Nutrition Information

Calories:250Kcal|Totalfat:19g|Saturatedfat:9g|Transfat:0g|Cholesterol:16
193mg|Carbohydrates: 2g|Sugar: 2g|Protein: 14g| Iron: 1mg| Calcium:
13mg

Air Fryer Breakfast Sweet Potato Skins

Prep Time:

7 Minutes Cook Time: 23 Minutes Total Time: 30 Minutes

Ingredients:

- 2 medium sweet potatoes 2 tsp. olive oil
- 4 eggs
- 1/4 c. whole milk salt and pepper
- 4 slices cooked bacon 2 green onions, sliced

Instructions:

- Wash the sweet potatoes and add 3-4 cuts to the potatoes. Microwave for 6-8 minutes, depending on their size until they are soft.

- Using an oven mitt, slice the potatoes in half lengthwise. Scoop out the potato flesh, leaving 1/4 inch around the edges. Save the scooped sweet potato for another use.

- Brush the potato skins with olive oil and sprinkle with sea salt. Arrange the skins in your Air Fryer basket and cook at 400° (or the highest available temp) for 10 minutes.

- Meanwhile, add the eggs, milk, salt, and pepper to a non-stick skillet. Cook the mixture over medium heat, stirring constantly, until there are no longer any visible liquid eggs.

- Top each cooked potato skin with 1/4 of the scrambled eggs and 1 slice of crumbled bacon. Cover with shredded cheese and cook for 3 minutes, or until the cheese is melted.

- Serve topped with green onion.

Nutritional Value:

Calories:208Kcal|Totalfat:12g|Saturatedfat:4g|Transfat:0g|Cholesterol:1367mg|Carbohydrates: 14g|Sugar: 5g|Protein: 12g| Iron: 2mg|

Air Fryer French Toast Sticks

Prep Time:

7 Minutes Cook Time: 8 Minutes Total Time: 15 Minutes

Ingredients:

- 12 slices Texas Toast 1 cup milk
- 5 large eggs
- 4 tbsp. butter, melted 1 tsp. vanilla extract
- 1/4 cup granulated sugar 1 tbsp. cinnamon
- Maple syrup, optional

Instructions:

- Slice each bread slice into thirds.

- In a bowl, add the milk, eggs, butter, and vanilla. Whisk until combined. In a separate bowl, add the cinnamon and sugar.

- Dip each breadstick quickly into the egg mixture. Sprinkle the sugar mixture onto both sides.

- Place into the air fryer basket and cook at 350°F for about 8 minutes until just crispy.

- Remove from basket and allow to cool. Serve with maple syrup, if desired.

Nutrition Information:

Calories: 170| Total Fat: 8g| Saturated Fat: 4g| Cholesterol: 90mg| Sodium: 183mg| Fiber: 1g| Sugar: 7g| Protein: 6g

Air Fryer Breakfast Taquitos Recipe

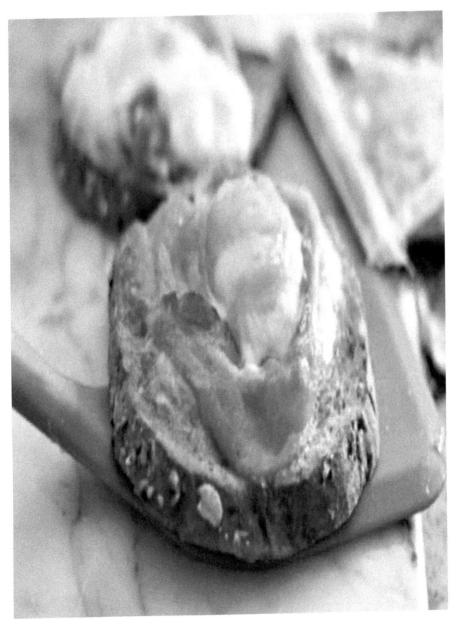

Prep Time:

25 mins Cook Time: 6 mins Total Time: 31 mins

Ingredients

- pound ground turkey sausage 2 teaspoons onion powder
- 2 cloves garlic minced
- ½ teaspoon salt
- ½ teaspoon pepper 6 large eggs
- 16 small low carb flour or whole wheat tortillas
- cup fat-free shredded Mexican blend or cheddar cheese 2 tablespoons Can't Believe It's Not Butter Melted

Instructions:

- Preheat oven to 400 F degrees. Lightly spray a 9x13 baking dish with coconut oil

- In a large skillet, cook sausage until it's is no longer pink. Drain. Add garlic and cook until soft. Season with onion powder, salt, and pepper. In a bowl, whisk eggs and pour into the skillet and cook until eggs are scrambled. Remove skillet from the stovetop. Add mixture to a bowl and set aside. Add tortillas to the microwave for 20 seconds. This softens them and makes it easier to roll them. On a flat surface, top a tortilla with 2 tablespoons of the skillet mixture. Top with a sprinkle of cheese. Roll the tortilla tightly and place in the baking dish. Brush with melted butter. Repeat until the remaining tortillas are filled. Pre-heat Air Fryer to 350° for 1 minute. Bake for 3 minutes and turn, and bake for an additional 2-3 minutes or until tortillas are golden brown and crispy.

- Serve with your favorite toppings!

Nutritional Facts:

Calories:178Kcal|Totalfat:15g|Saturatedfat:8g|Transfat:12g|Cholesterol:194 193mg|Carbohydrates: 2g|Sugar: 1g|Protein: 5g| Iron: 0.8mg| Calcium: 25mg : 112mg | Vitamin A: 21IU | Calcium: 3mg | Iron: 1mg

Air Fryer Egg Cups

Prep Time:

5 minutes Cook Time: 12 minutes Total Time: 17 minutes Yield: 8

Ingredients:

- 6 large eggs
- 1/2 cup of heavy cream (use low-fat milk for WW) 1/2 cup of cheddar
- 1/2 pound of breakfast sausage 1 tsp of olive oil
- tsp of garlic
- cups of spinach

Instructions:

- Heat a nonstick skillet to medium-low.

- Add ground breakfast sausage and cook for 12-16 minutes or until cooked through and browned. Crumble the sausage with a wooden spoon or cooking utensil of choice.

- Remove the breakfast sausage from the skillet. Let the sausage cool. Add 1 tsp of olive oil and garlic to the skillet. Cook until the garlic is fragrant and Add the spinach to the skillet and cover; allow to cook 5 minutes. Take the spinach out of the pan let it cool as you did with the sausage.

- In a medium bowl add the eggs and milk and whisk until combined. Fold in the cheddar, breakfast sausage, and spinach.

- Place the silicone muffin cups into the air fryer basket and set the temperature to 300 degrees. Fill the cups with the egg mixture (do no overfill). I used a measuring cup to fill the muffin cups.

- Set the air fryer time to 12 minutes.

- I had egg mixture left over after only cooking six egg cups at a time. My air fryer basket only fit 6 muffin cups in there without overflowin Will have to cook in batches if there is any leftover.

Nutrition Value:

Calories:230|Sugar:1g|Fat:19g|Sat Fat: 7g|Unsaturated Fat: 4g|Carbohydrates:

4g| Fiber: 0g| Protein: 10g

Air Fryer Quiche

Prep Time:

10 minutes Cook time: 10 minutes Total time: 20 minutes Yield: makes 1

Ingredients:

- 1 egg
- 3-4 tbsp (45ml-60ml) of heavy cream 4-5 tiny broccoli florets
- 1 tbsp (15ml) finely grated cheddar cheese

Instructions:

- Whisk together egg and cream. Lightly grease a 5" (13cm) ceramic quiche dish. Distribute broccoli florets on the bottom. Pour in the egg mixture. Top with grated cheddar cheese.

- Air fry at 325F (162C) for 10 minutes.

- More Air Fryer Quiche Fillings:

- Tomato and Mozzarella. Garnish with fresh basil Spinach and Cheese

- Cooked bacon and Cheddar Mushroom and Thyme Smoked Salmon and Dill

- Goat Cheese and Crispy Leeks (cook leeks first in a skillet with olive oil until crispy)

Nutrition Information:

Calories: 656| Total Fat: 58g| Saturated Fat: 34g| Trans Fat: 2g| Unsaturated Fat: 19g| Cholesterol: 349mg| Sodium: 364mg| Carbohydrates: 18g| Fiber: 6g| Sugar: 6g| Protein: 21g

Vegan Air Fryer Breakfast Potatoes

Prep Time:

0 minutes Cook Time: 40 minutes Total Time: 40 minutes

Ingredients:

- 3 lb potatoes, diced
- 2 bell peppers, any color, diced 1 onion, diced
- 15 oz mushrooms, diced
- 1/2 cups or 1-14 oz can black beans, drained Lemon Miso Tahini Sauc optional
- Spinach and avocado for serving, optional

Instructions:

- IF AIR FRYING: Add potatoes to the air fryer basket. Cook 20 minutes at 400 degrees F (or 205 degrees C), shaking basket frequently.

- Add beans and vegetables and cook 10 - 15 more minutes until potatoes are soft or crispy, according to preference.

- IF BAKING: Spread potatoes out on a lined baking tray and bake for 25-30 minutes in a 425 degree F (218 degrees C) oven.

- Remove the tray and flip the potatoes. Add your veggies and beans and stir. Put the tray back in the oven for 15-20 more minutes, until the potatoes have started to get crispy and lightly golden brown and until all the veggies have cooked.

- Make the lemon miso tahini sauce by mixing the ingredients in a bowl and thinning the sauce with water if needed.

- Add to a bowl with spinach and whatever else you like (this would be a great complement to tofu scramble, for instance). Top with sauce mixture and enjoy!

- Refrigerate leftovers in an airtight container for up to 5 days. Recommended reheating in the oven, skillet, or air fryer to retain crispiness.

Nutritional Value:

Calories: 164 Total Fat: 0.5g Sodium: 200.5g

Total carbohydrate: 34.7g

Sugar: 4g Protein: 7.2g

Fried Eggs For The Air Fryer

Prep Time:

1 Minute Cook Time: 8 Minutes Total Time: 9 Minutes

Ingredients

- Large Eggs
- 2 Tablespoons Butter Salt And Pepper

Instructions:

- Add a small aluminum pan to the basket of an air fryer.

- Add the butter and heat at 350 degrees to melt (approximately 1 minute) Crack both eggs into the aluminum pan.

- Return to the air fryer and cook at 325-degrees until your desired doneness.

Nutrition Information:

Calories: 363 Total Fat: 33g Saturated Fat: 18g

Cholesterol: 482mg

Sodium: 361mg Carbohydrates: 1g Sugar: 1g

Protein: 14g

Turkey Breakfast Sausage - Air Fryer O Oven Method

Prep Time:

5 Minutes Cook Time: 13 Minutes Total Time: 18 Minutes

Ingredients:

- 1 pound ground turkey 1 teaspoon kosher salt
- ½ teaspoon black pepper 1 teaspoon fennel seed
- ½ teaspoon ground sage
- ½ teaspoon smoked paprika 3/4 teaspoon garlic powder
- 1/8 teaspoon red pepper flakes (or to taste)

Instructions:

- Place all the ingredients in a medium bowl and mix well to combine. Wet hands with water and form the ground turkey mixture into 12-13 small patties (approximately 1½ tablespoons, each).

- Place the patties on an air fryer baking sheet and cook for 12-13 minutes at 350-degrees (or until an instant-read thermometer reached 165-degrees when inserted into the center of a sausage.

Nutrition Information:

Calories: 91 Total Fat: 6g Saturated Fat: 2g

Unsaturated Fat: 4g Cholesterol: 37mg Sodium: 193mg Protein: 9g

Dry Rub Skirt Steak Sandwiches

Prep Time:

10 Minutes Cook Time: 15 Minutes Inactive Time: 30 Minutes Total Time
55 Minutes

Ingredients:

- For The Dry Rub

- 3 tablespoons ground coriander 3 tablespoons smoked paprika

- 3 tablespoons ground smoked cumin 1 teaspoon allspice

- 1½ tablespoons ground cinnamon 2 tablespoons dried oregano

- 1½ tablespoons dry mustard 3 tablespoons salt

- 1½ tablespoons black pepper 2 tablespoons garlic powder 4
  tablespoons brown sugar For the sandwich

- 2 beef skirt steaks

- 1 tablespoon canola oil

- 3 green bell peppers, seeded and sliced 2 large sweet onions, peeled
  and sliced

- ½ teaspoon salt

- ¼ teaspoon pepper 8 crusty rolls

- 1½ cup beef broth for dipping, optional hot sauce, optional

Instructions:

- In a large bowl with a lid, mix all the ingredients for the dry rub until well combined.

- Place the meat on the baking sheet and liberally sprinkle the dry rub on both sides of the meat and rub it in lightly.

- Allow the meat to sit for approximately 30 minutes.

- Meanwhile, heat a large skillet to medium, add the canola oil and the sliced peppers and onions.

- Sautee the green peppers and onions with ½ teaspoon salt and ¼ pepper until they softened and cooked through. Remove from heat and keep warm.

- Place the steaks on a hot grill and cook for approximately 5 minutes per side.

- Remove the cooked steaks from the grill and allow them to sit, covered with aluminum foil, for at least 10 minutes.

- Slice the meat across the grain in thin slices.

- To serve pile the sliced beef onto crusty rolls and top with the sauteed peppers and onions.

- Spoon (or dip) the beef stock over the prepared sandwiches and a few shakes of hot sauce if desired.

- Serve hot!

Nutrition Information::

Calories: 399 Total Fat: 17g

Saturated Fat: 5g

Trans Fat: 0g Unsaturated Fat: 10g Cholesterol: 64mg Sodium: 3218mg Carbohydrates: 37g Fiber: 7g

Sugar: 13g Protein: 27g

Air Fryer French Toast

Prep Time:

5 mins Cook Time: 9 mins Total Time: 14 mins

Ingredients:

- eggs
- 2 TBS milk, cream, or half and half 1/2 tsp ground cinnamon
- 1/2 tsp vanilla extract
- 1 loaf challah or brioche bread, cut into 8 thick slices

Instructions:

- In a medium bowl, add egg, milk, vanilla, and cinnamon; whisk to combine completely; set aside

- Make an assembly line: set up whisked egg mixture and bread next to each other.

- Spray the air fryer basket with nonstick oil spray

- Dip the slices of bread into the egg mixture being sure to flip and coat both sides. Lift out of the mixture and allow to drip for a few seconds, then place into the air fryer basket. Repeat for remaining slices

- Close the Air Fryer. Set to 400 degrees and 5 minutes. After 5 minutes, open the basket and carefully flip the french toast slices. Close the air fryer and cook for 3-4 more minutes at 400 degrees. *Time may vary slightly depending on the air fryer model.

- Remove the french toast when finished and then cook the remaining french toast slices.

- Serve with warm maple syrup and powdered sugar or your favorite toppings!

Nutrition Facts:

Calories:150Kcal|Totalfat:12g|Saturatedfat:4g|Transfat:0g|Cholesterol:1 200mg|Carbohydrates: 4g|Sugar: 1g|Protein: 3g| Iron: 2mg|

Air Fryer Breakfast Pockets

Prep Time:

30 minutes Cook Time: 15 minutes

Ingredients:

- 1 lb of ground pork 4 whole eggs
- whole egg for egg wash 1/3 + 1/4 c of whole milk
- 1-2 ounces of Velveeta cheese Salt and pepper to taste
- packages of Pillsbury pie crust 2 crusts to a package 2-gallon ziplock bags
- parchment paper Cooking spray

Instructions:

- Remove pie crusts from the refrigerator. Brown and drain the pork.

- Heat 1/4 c milk and cheese in a small pot until melted.

- Whisk 4 eggs, season with salt and pepper, and add remaining milk. Scramble eggs in a skillet until almost fully cooked.

- Mix the meat, cheese, and eggs.

- Roll out your pie crust and cut it into a 3-4 inch circle (about the size of a cereal bowl).

- Whisk one egg to make an egg wash.

- Place about 2 tbsps of mix into the middle of each circle. Egg wash all edges of the circle.

- Fold the circle creating a moon shape. Crimp the folded edges with a fork.

- Layer the pockets in parchment paper and place them in a plastic ziplock bag overnight.

- Once ready to cook, pre-heat your Air Fryer to 360 degrees. Spray each side of the pocket with cooking spray.

- Place pockets in pre-heated Air Fryer for 15 minutes or until golden brown.

- Remove from Air Fryer and allow to cool for a few minutes before serving.

Nutrition Facts:

Calories:140Kcal|Totalfat:15g|Saturatedfat:8g|Transfat:2g|Cholesterol:1 180mg|Carbohydrates: 2g|Sugar:2g|Protein: 10g| Iron: 2mg| Calcium: 13mg

Air Fryer Cheesy Baked Eggs

Prep Time:

4 minutes Cook Time: 16 minutes Total Time: 20 minutes Servings: 2

Ingredients:

- 4 large Eggs
- ounces Smoked gouda, chopped Everything bagel seasoning
- Salt and pepper to taste

Instructions:

- Spray the inside of each ramekin with cooking spray. Add 2 eggs to each ramekin, then add 1 ounce of chopped gouda to each. Salt and pepper to taste. Sprinkle your everything bagel seasoning on top of each ramekin (as much as you like). Place each ramekin into the air fryer basket. Cook for 400F for 16 minutes, or until eggs are cooked through. Serve.

Nutrition:

Calories: 240kcal | Carbohydrates: 1g | Protein: 12g | Fat: 16g

Low-Carb Air Fryer Bacon And Egg Cup

Prep Time:

10 Minutes Cook Time: 10 Minutes Total Time: 20 Minutes

Ingredients:

- slices bacon, sliced in half 6 large eggs
- 1 bunch green onions, optional salt and pepper, optional

Instructions:

- Arrange 6 baking cups (silicone or paper) in the air fryer basket. Spray with nonstick cooking spray.

- Line cups with bacon slice. Carefully crack an egg into each cup. Season with salt and pepper, if desired.

- Turn the air fryer on to 330° and cook for 10 minutes, until eggs are set. Carefully remove from air fryer and garnish with desired toppings.

Nutrition Information:

Calories:115Kcal|Totalfat:9g|Saturatedfat:3g|Transfat:0g|Cholesterol:10 160mg|Carbohydrates: 0g|Sugar: 0g|Protein: 8g| Iron: 2mg|

Air Fryer English Breakfast

Prep Time:

3 mins Cook Time: 15 mins Total Time:18 mins

Ingredients:

- 6 English Sausages
- 6 Bacon Rashers
- 2 Large Tomatoes
- 4 Black Pudding
- ½ Can Baked Beans 2 Large Eggs
- 1 Tbsp Whole Milk 1 Tsp Butter
- Salt & Pepper

Instructions:

- Crack your eggs into a ramekin and stir in butter, milk, and salt and pepper. Place in the air fryer. Add to the air fryer bacon rashers, black pudding, and sausages. Slice tomatoes in half and season the top with salt and pepper.

- Close the air fryer basket, making sure first that there is room for each of the breakfast items to cook. Then cook for 10 minutes at 180c/360f. Though at the 5-minute interval stir your eggs with a fork.

- When the air fryer beeps, check to make sure the eggs are scrambled and remove the scrambled eggs with a kitchen glove or kitchen tongs. Replace the ramekin space with a ramekin of cold baked beans. Cook for a further 5 minutes at the same temperature.

- When it beeps load your English breakfast ingredients onto a plate and enjoy.

Nutrition:

Calories: 1496kcal | Carbohydrates: 22g | Protein: 70g | Fat: 124g | Saturated Fat: 42g | Cholesterol: 463mg | Sodium: 3005mg | Potassium: 1564mg | Fiber: 6g | Sugar: 4g | Vitamin A: 1579IU | Vitamin C: 21mg | Calcium: 117mg | Iron: 6mg

Air Fryer Bacon And Egg Toast

Prep Time:

1 Minute Cook Time: 9 Minutes Total Time: 10 Minutes

Ingredients:

- Butter (if desired) 1 slice of bread
- 1 slice of bacon 1 egg
- Salt & pepper to taste

Directions:

- Butter a slice of bread and place it in the air fryer. Add a slice of bacon around the top of the bread. Add an egg in the middle.

- Close the air fryer and cook for 9 minutes at 340 degrees, or until the desired doneness. Salt & pepper to taste. Enjoy!

Nutritional Value:

Calories:178Kcal|Totalfat:15g|Saturatedfat:8g|Transfat:0g|Cholesterol:1 193mg|Carbohydrates: 2g|Sugar: 1g|Protein: 5g| Iron: 0.8mg| Calcium: 25mg

How To Make Bacon In Your Air Fryer

Prep Time:

5 minutes Cook Time: 10 minutes

Ingredients:

- Basic Air Fryer Bacon

- 4 pieces of thick-cut bacon 2 eggs

- tablespoon butter

- croissants sliced 1/2 cup ketchup

- 2 tablespoons apple cider vinegar 1 tablespoon molasses

- 1 tablespoon brown sugar 1/4 teaspoon mustard powder 1/4 teaspoon onion powder

- 1/2 tablespoon Worcestershire sauce 1/4 teaspoon liquid smoke

Instructions:

- Basic Air Fryer Bacon

- Preheat your Air fryer to 200 degrees C (or 390 degrees F) Lay the bacon strips of your choice flat on the Air fryer tray. Cook for 4-5 minutes, then flip the bacon.

- Cook for another 4-5 minutes until the desired doneness is reached. Air Fryer Bacon With BBQ Sauce Croissants

- Preheat your Air fryer to 200 degrees C (or 390 degrees F)

- Whisk together in a small saucepan the ketchup, apple cider vinegar, molasses, brown sugar, mustard powder, onion powder, Worcestershire sauce, and liquid smoke. Place on medium heat and bring to a simmer, cooking until the sauce thickens slightly.

- Lay the bacon flat on the Airfryer tray and brush with BBQ sauce. Cook for 4-5 minutes, then flip the bacon and brush the other side of the bacon with sauce. Cook for an additional 5 minutes or until the desired doneness is reached.

- Place the croissants into your toaster and toast lightly.

- Melt the butter in a medium-sized frying pan and fry the eggs until they reach your desired doneness. (over-easy is best).

- Place an egg on the bottom of one croissant, followed by two bacon

- slices and the croissant top. Repeat with the other croissant. Serve and enjoy!

Nutrition Information:

Calories: 656kcal, Carbohydrates: 57g, Protein: 16g, Fat: 39g, Saturated Fat: 17g, Cholesterol: 246mg, Sodium: 1262mg, Potassium: 584mg, Fiber: 1g, Sugar: 33g, Vitamin A: 1145IU, Vitamin C: 3mg, Calcium: 76mg, Iron: 3mg

Air Fryer Bacon

Prep Time:

2 Minutes Cook Time: 10 Minutes Total Time: 12 Minutes

Ingredients:

*   8 ounces bacon about 8 strips Water

Instructions:

- Preheat the air fryer at 350F for about 5 minutes.

- Pour ¼ cup of water into the bottom of the air fryer to minimize smoke. Make sure the water is not touching the basket or bacon. (You can also place a layer of bread in the bottom of the air fryer.)

- Place bacon in a single layer into the preheated air fryer basket. Feel free to cut bacon strips in half or even in thirds to make it fit nicely.

- Cook for 8 to 10 minutes for thinner bacon and 12 to 15 minutes for thicker cut bacon.

Nutrition:

Calories: 236kcal | Carbohydrates: 1g | Protein: 7g | Fat: 23g | Saturated Fat: 8g | Cholesterol: 37mg | Sodium: 375mg | Potassium

Fryer Mini Breakfast Burritos

Prep Time:

15 mins Cook Time: 30 mins Total Time: 45 mins

Ingredient:

- ¼ cup Mexican-style chorizo 1 tablespoon bacon grease
- ½ cup diced potatoes
- 2 tablespoons chopped onion 1 serrano pepper, chopped
- 2 large eggs
- Salt and ground black pepper to taste 4 (8 inches) flour tortillas
- Avocado oil cooking spray

Instructions:

- Cook chorizo in a large skillet over medium-high heat, stirring frequently until sausage turns a dark red, 6 to 8 minutes. Remove from the skillet and set aside.

- Melt bacon grease in the same skillet over medium-high heat. Add diced potatoes and cook, stirring occasionally, 8 to 10 minutes. Add onion and serrano pepper and continue cooking and stirring until potatoes are fork-tender, onion is translucent, and serrano pepper is soft, 2 to 6 minutes. Add eggs and chorizo; stir until cooked and completely incorporated into potato mixture, about 5 minutes. Season with salt and pepper.

- Meanwhile, heat tortillas in a large skillet or directly on the grates of a gas stove until soft and pliable. Place 1/3 cup chorizo mixture down the center of each tortilla. Fold top and bottom of tortillas over the filling, then roll each into a burrito shape. Mist with cooking spray and place in the basket of an air fryer.

- Air fry at 400 degrees F (200 degrees C) for 4 to 6 minutes. Flip each burrito over, mist with cooking spray, and air fry until lightly browned, 2 to 4 minutes more.

Nutritional Value:

Calories: 253.8

Protein: 8.3g Carbohydrates: 31.4g Dietary Fiber: 2.2g Sugars: 0.6g

Fat: 10.4g Saturated Fat: 3.3g

Cholesterol: 98.1mg Vitamin B6: 0.1mg Vitamin C: 4.9mg Folate: 76.5mcg Calcium: 36.1mg Iron: 2.3mg Magnesium: 21.4mg Potassium: 198.4mg Sodium: 298.2mg

Fryer Churros

Prep Time:

5 mins Cook Time: 15 mins Additional Time: 5 mins Total Time: 25 mins

Ingredient:

- ¼ cup butter
- ½ cup milk 1 pinch salt
- ½ cup all-purpose flour 2 eggs
- ¼ cup white sugar
- ½ teaspoon ground cinnamon

Instructions:

- Melt butter in a saucepan over medium-high heat. Pour in milk and add salt. Lower heat to medium and bring to a boil, continuously stirring with a wooden spoon. Quickly add flour all at once. Keep stirring until the dough comes together.

- Remove from heat and let cool for 5 to 7 minutes. Mix in eggs with the wooden spoon until the pastry comes together. Spoon dough into a pastry bag fitted with a large star tip. Pipe dough into strips straight into the air fryer basket.

- Air fry churros at 340 degrees F (175 degrees C) for 5 minutes. Meanwhile, combine sugar and cinnamon in a small bowl and pour onto a shallow plate.

- Remove fried churros from the air fryer and roll in the cinnamon-sugar mixture.

Nutrition Facts:

Protein: 3.9g Carbohydrates: 17.5g Dietary Fiber: 0.4g Sugars: 9.4g

Fat: 9.8g Saturated Fat: 5.6g Cholesterol: 84mg

Vitamin A Iu: 356.5IU Niacin Equivalents: 1.5mg Folate: 28.2mcg

Calcium: 38.5mg Iron: 0.8mg Magnesium: 6.8mg Potassium: 67.2mg Sodium: 112.2mg Thiamin: 0.1mg

Calories From Fat: 88.5

Alphabetical Index

A

B

CPSIA information can be obtained
at www.ICGtesting.com
Printed in the USA
LVHW081201270521
688664LV00006B/661